DON'T ASK
PERMISSION TO FLY

———

The following is included with permission by Employment Resources, Inc. (ERI) (www.eri-wi.org). Some of the essays in this collection are based on content that was funded by ERI. The ideas, opinions, and conclusions expressed are those of Anna Gouker and do not necessarily represent recommendations, endorsements, or policies of ERI.

Don't Ask Permission to

fly

by Anna Gouker

————

To the unstoppable force,

J E S L

The future is in your hands.

————

CONTENTS

INTRODUCTION

Dear You,

Let's not beat around the bush. I'm someone who was born knowing everything... or there was a time when I thought so. I was six years old when my parents bought their first house. We moved into a bigger place that allowed me to have my own bedroom, bumping up my status in this world. I distinctly recall the feeling that I was fully ready to live on my own. The experiences of interacting with other kids at school and hitting the brick wall of adolescence did their job of knocking that know-it-all attitude right out of me. No matter how turbulent the ride is, I'm a person who always gets up and finds a way to move forward.

Skipping ahead to 28, I had just gotten my first job as I sat in my favorite restaurant and told the bartender in my most genuinely surprised voice, "I started a rumor a long time ago that I'm awesome and I think it's really starting to catch on!"

It wasn't. You'll find out what happened with that job later.

As I'm writing this, I'm elbows-deep in my 30s. I'm more cognitively aware of all the things I don't yet know or understand about life, but my conviction is stronger than ever that having a solid connection to who I am is the most important thing. It's a tricky thing to be a complex person in a world that likes to oversimplify everyone in it. Each of us moves so quickly through this busy, tech-centered, results-based life that we don't always realize we allowed others to push, prod, and mold us right into boxes that make no sense for the reality of who we are. Look, we are social creatures. I accept that. Labels, teams, and tribes – these are the mechanisms we use to make connections. And, in certain ways, it's important that we embrace that part of our nature. It's the ill-informed assumptions we make about each other that's the problem. When people look at me, they see my physical traits and think they know the full story. They don't. And that's when the helpful mechanisms of our species become defects. I'm an individual with unique gifts to share. I won't be pushed into someone else's false impression of me. If I lose touch of what's true about me, I won't be able to reach the extent of my true capability.

Growing up, the path was unclear. At the time, I didn't personally know or know of any adults who mirrored my idea of success. There was no one who I could latch onto as a target for my own hopes and dreams. Instead, I looked to fiction. The best example is "Alias," a TV show about Sydney Bristow, a Girl Next Door type of twentysomething, devoting her attention to her close friendships and pushing towards her grad degree in literature, struggling to balance it all while maintaining a secret career in US Intelligence.

The show aired when I was a teenager and I was introduced to Agent Bristow at exactly the right time. My real life has always been full of strong female characters, but this one gave me a license to use the heightened framework in which I view my life. I watched her jet setting the globe, fighting terrorists, executing covert operations, and making the world a safer place – even her academic pursuit depicted as the ultimate act of rebellion, her diploma offering evidence of the talents she held outside her profession. Few people in her orbit can see the full picture of her, yet the audience is in on the whole thing; Sydney's a good-natured friend and student with a fearless attitude and unmatched ability to take down the biggest and baddest super villains.

Meanwhile, I was living out my own kind of split existence. Going to school during the day surrounded by peers who didn't know if I could speak and didn't care to find out, then bounding home to get back to the work of planning and dreaming for the big, bright future I had ahead of me. I didn't know what it was going to look like or which profession I would be in – I feverishly hopscotched from one idea to the next: fashion designer, criminal profiler, and then there was that brief phase where I saw potential in becoming an inspirational Prison Warden – those were just details. Without evidence that could be found on my report card, in any of my standardized test results, or sampled and examined under a microscope, I knew I had something substantial inside of me waiting to be used in service of a cause bigger than myself.

Over the years, new characters have come into my life – we don't need to go into each of them here or talk about all the ways I feel like I'm Batman – all the while, my own perceptions have evolved. With the fictitious people I have connected to, I have developed a new understanding of how someone like me can effectively move in this world ... which brings me to you. My wish for you is to absorb the stories contained in this book of essays, the protagonist being a real human woman, understanding that she may as well be you. Just as you will find in these tales, each day is an opportunity—for fear, confusion, failure, self-discovery, excellence, or all of the above. No one understands you or the gifts you have to offer better than you. This is your life. Whatever path you find yourself on, know that it is yours to choose.

> *If you're always trying*
> *to be normal, you will never know*
> *how amazing you can be.*

—MAYA ANGELOU

WELCOME TO
THE GOOD LIFE

———

After completing my master's degree, I imagined I was being shot out of the dull, stuffy world of academia and into the vibrant arena of employment–ready to make my mark. Finally, at age 27, I began each day with knowing confidence. After many years of trying to stay awake, bundled up inside overly air-conditioned classrooms, the gifts, talents, and desires that I was born with were about to guide me straight to my destiny. I was sure of it.

I was also sure that sleeping until noon—or 1, or 2, or 3—was a new kind of comfortable routine, following regular late nights of submitting job applications and rewriting my CV. On one such afternoon—almost-evening—I was ready for my daily caffeine fix. At that time, my coffee intake had likewise become its own kind of ritual. One that provided two types of stimulants: the regular social interaction I needed to stay sane and the brewed beverage that I never stop craving. Aside from my weekly volunteer Bingo commitment at the local community center, my newfound life as a non-student, or whatever you would call a young professional who has never worked a job, didn't offer many reasons to leave my apartment. The aroma of coffee, or even the *memory* of the aroma of coffee, has—and probably always will—motivate me to go just about anywhere. I had almost reached the coffee bar inside my neighborhood grocery store when a very well-intentioned woman approached me.

"Can I pray with you?" she asked.

"Sure!" I agreed.

I never want to reject someone else's interest in bringing an extra dose of positive energy into my life. A good prayer from a light-hearted stranger seemed like the right compliment to my coffee. What I got was something else entirely. As tears filled her eyes, she called on Jesus to make her a vessel for His healing. Yet again, I was confronted with the notion that I—a seemingly helpless figure with a hushed voice in a motorized wheelchair—come off as tragic to other people.

This woman and her snap assumptions were now conspiring to block me from the iced caramel latte that I was desperately craving.

All I could think was, *Stupid, me.* It was me who had agreed to this awkward exchange with the firm belief that humans should all be cheerleaders for one another, embracing the invisible connection that bonds us. It was too late before I realized the reality of this encounter: I was to play the part of the helpless girl as she offered a theatrical performance of pity for all to see.

At that moment, a whole bank of memories flooded back to me—moments I had stuffed away over time. Like when I was about 10 years old, partaking in my town's annual summer festival—or at least trying to—as my father and I were approached by three ladies asking to pray for me. They seemed harmless. But, amongst the flashing Ferris wheel lights and hordes of laughing children gripping cotton candy and guppy fish like trophies, I found myself momentarily held captive by a swarm of sobbing adults. Now I'm an adult myself, yet I am still routinely trapped by others who perceive my life to be a tragedy. That's not how I see it.

Tragedy is when I make choices that prevent my progress, hindering me from becoming the truest, fullest version of myself.

We all battle tragedy in this form from time to time. We all have bad habits and toxic relationships that are difficult to end, or tendencies that lead to unhappiness. Yet the cycle of behavior can just keep repeating. It's a tragedy when we find ourselves moving toward bad yet comfortable choices, building walls and self-imposed limitations along the way. My wheelchair, which praying ladies see as a sign of weakness, is actually a symbol of liberation. My wheelchair should be celebrated for the miraculous feat of engineering that it is. It's the motor behind my drive and it literally and figuratively allows me to move forward every day.

I started on this road at a very young age. When I was eight months old, I was diagnosed with a genetic condition called Spinal Muscular Atrophy (SMA). SMA causes progressive muscle weakness throughout the body. I've never been able to walk. As I moved through adolescence, my arms and hands transformed from expressive to limp. The muscles that control my breathing are destined for failure. I get extremely winded if I speak for more than two or three minutes without stopping to rest, and that's on a good day. When I have a cold, on the other hand, normal life comes to a screeching halt. All other activities are wiped from my agenda. My entire existence consolidates into a single goal: to fill my lungs with air again. Clearing congestion from my lungs is made possible by several wondrous ventilator devices.

While technology and medical research are allowing people like me to live longer and fuller lives, my struggles are very real. I can't shrug off the fact that my ongoing battle to breathe is a big one and, because of my mobility impairment, everything I do takes more time than it would for your average young adult lady. I not only accept these challenges—I appreciate them. There are more benefits than limitations from these complexities.

Over the years, I have learned to fight—fight to keep this journey going as long as I can and fight for what I want to get out of my time here. I'm focused. I've met amazing people, and I appreciate what they have contributed to my life. I know how to have fun in almost everything I do. I've experienced extreme highs and devastating lows. I don't know what people mean when they refer to me as "wheelchair-bound," but to me, it's only confirmation that *I am limitless.*

So, the moral of the story is that I'm in the middle of a pretty beautiful adventure. Now, if you would like to do something to help me, do not get in between me and my coffee.

"

You gain strength, courage, and confidence by every experience in which you really stop to look fear in the face ... Do the thing you think you cannot do.

—ELEANOR ROOSEVELT

LOVE & LIGHT

On the day I realized that life was mine to conquer, I was five years old. I was tooling around our driveway in my older brother's motorized wheelchair—I didn't yet have my own, I moved up, then down, and in figure-eight formations.

Everything was lovely. Under the bright, warm sun, I felt like I was being swallowed up by a chair that was too big for my tiny frame. All of the elements synchronized to offer a comforting embrace. Birds chirped gleefully. Even the bees buzzing around seemed to be cheering me on as I performed my four-wheeled tricks.

The party ended abruptly. My front right wheel hit a crack in the pavement. I was certain that the Earth had tipped from its axis. My head fell off balance and slipped from its support rest. Mere seconds from the place I had been floating in pure harmony with the universe around me, I realized a new, sudden dark reality. My head hung to the side, my chin resting on my left shoulder. My mom, my only shining salvation, was inside the house. I was all alone.

Only a very small fragment of my child-sized brain knew that everything was going to be okay. My mom would surely be back outside very soon. But the rest of my brain screamed *PANIC!* I tried to call for her, but my words were now muffled. With my neck strained to the side, my vocal cords couldn't do their usual magic. In this state of stress and discomfort, I realized that my right hand could still reach the toggle switch to operate the chair. I spun around to see if any of my neighbors were outside. No one was there to notice me. I was truly alone. *What could these stupid bee friends do for me now?* I thought. I struggled to breathe and to swallow. I felt disconnected from the serenity and security of my mother's love.

Then a lightbulb flashed on. I had a chance. Parked in the driveway was the coolest thing my mom owned—a 1976 Ford Mustang. This wasn't one that you would have seen sported by John Travolta singing "Grease Lightning." No, this was a brown beauty with a tan roof—much more fitting for someone with my mom's subdued, quiet style. Unfortunately, it had to be sacrificed to release me from this fiasco. Despite my young age, I knew two things: I was in trouble, and I was being raised to be a woman of action.

I backed up to clear about 10 feet for maximum velocity. Then I sped forward, the front right edge of my wheelchair colliding full force into the Mustang's back bumper, careful not to smash my shins in an act of collateral damage. To my horror, the sound from the crash was more like a stick snapping than the earthquake-like rumble I had imagined—the kind of commotion that would automatically prompt a response from the entire neighborhood. I waited. Surely, someone was about to reveal themselves. A good Samaritan would come outside to see what was going on. Anyone.

Although I had endured a jolt in my act of desperation, there was not much of a ruckus to be heard.

A minute later, out of divine intervention—or total coincidence—my saintly mother emerged from the front door of our house. Seeing her, knowing she would put me back in my rightful vertical position, was like the breath of life rushing back into me. With her, I had always been fearless. Without her, I was in the dark. But my biggest concern at that point was explaining what happened to the Mustang.

Since then, I've hit many potholes concealed by shadows, throwing my plans off course. Time and time again, I've been struck by the understanding that though my muscles have always been weak, I come from the woman who defined strength for me. She gave me more than comfort and security. Her insistence on my success—the vision she has always held for me—carries me forward. She is the reason I can't be rattled.

I inherited from my mom a light that lives inside of me, shining on solutions to my obstacles. The reflection of her brilliance guides me on my path.

> **We know what we are,
> but not what we may be.**
>
> —WILLIAM SHAKESPEARE

SADDLE UP

———

Time isn't money. Time is discovery. And when I was fourteen, I made a big one —Madonna. She and I had both been around for a while by that point, but my exposure was limited. Her rebellious attitude clicked with me, but she always felt a bit out of reach. Many of the cultural references associated with her were from the '80s and '90's—eras I don't fully connect with. But when I saw the music video for her 2000 single "Don't Tell Me," the Material Girl finally offered something I could get behind. In the rugged yet glamorous video, Madonna wears ripped blue jeans, plaid, and gemstones in the Wild West. My adolescent brain hadn't before considered this beautiful combination! In the song, Madonna declares that she will not be told whom or how to love.

Loving with freedom and living with freedom are one and the same. Living in a tiny Midwestern town, my high school survival guide was defiance. Not resisting authority, but methodically pushing against the mold that others thought I should fit into. At a young age, I realized that to move forward, I had to identify the difference between who I really was and who others told me I was.

I needed to reject the assumptions, expectations, and ideals that others projected on me and focus on what I knew to be true about myself.

Moving through high school at the beginning of the 21st Century was less challenging than American frontier life—less dysentery, more social pressure. But hope for survival sometimes felt just as grim. All discovery takes grit. In high school, the stakes could not be higher. For any cowgirl, learning about who you are and how your unique quirks and talents fit into the world around you is a never-ending process. Disability adds an extra level of complexity. Of course, there are benefits to developing sacred bonds with wonderful caregivers, teachers, occupational therapists, physical therapists, etc., whom I wouldn't have known otherwise. But disability also created roadblocks between me and where I wanted to be. High school survival is all about fitting into the social framework and finding 'your people.' Even in movies about high school, the geeks and social outcasts gravitate towards each other and transform into heroes by the end of the story. But my people were the adults.

During senior year, I left class for an hour each week to meet with my speech therapist. One day, I was feeling especially disheartened by my inability to connect with my peers. As tears rolled down my cheeks, I told her how the other students didn't look me in the eye. Teen years are a crucial time for making connections. I thought my path was being shaped by others' limited perceptions of me. I thought this was the beginning of a never-ending downward slump. I saw my classmates as the gatekeepers to the life I wanted. I was afraid they were deciding my fate and future. Adult life was the new frontier, and I did not yet see what was on the horizon.

While sitting through progress meetings with my family, faculty, and school administrators, it was clear that few people envisioned my future the way I did—living on my own and making a contribution through meaningful work. Though I had a whole team helping me craft my life as I entered adulthood, I often felt very alone in my vision.

I finished high school over 15 years ago. Since then, I have gone to college and completed a master's degree, moved to a new city in a new state, and entered the workforce. Even now, I frequently encounter subtle hints from others that, because of my disability, I should spend my days at home. A life where I am just trying to survive is not a life for me. I'm not done discovering my truth and setting the terms for my life, resisting the expectations of others in every way. Nobody knows where this rocky terrain will take me, and that is part of the beauty that I can see.

Tell me love isn't true
It's just something that we do
Tell me everything I'm not
But please don't tell me to stop

—"Don't Tell Me" by Madonna*

*In case of any legal issue with reprinting these lyrics, Madonna can contact me via annagouker.com

"

*Today is the first day of
the rest of your life.*

—JOHN DENVER

REMOVING THE
VOICE OF DOUBT

He looked right at me and said, "What do you think of feminism?"

I was sitting in the empty area in front of the front row of students. That is where you would find me in most classrooms, the only location I could fit my comfy, bulky, technologically advanced chair, an ironic fact because at that time, it was my purpose in life to take up as little space as possible. The sudden spotlight on me gave a jolt of anxiety in my stomach. My sociology instructor had just done the unthinkable—he had shattered the invisible wall I had been peacefully existing behind.

On a regular school day, driving the 40 minutes back and forth from my home to class was an ordeal in itself, let alone all of the disruptive events that could happen in between. As a 19-year-old community college student, I strived for perfect attendance—and often achieved it. But doing so meant clearing whatever unexpected hurdles popped up throughout each day. I was accustomed to unpredictable health and a variety of surprises that come with managing a caregiver schedule. Each sunrise brought an opportunity for victory, a problem ready to be solved, or a crisis that needed to be dodged. And then I tried to do some learning with whatever energy I had left. With all of these rogue variables, I didn't feel bad about demurring from classroom discussions. So, this introvert was caught by surprise when Mr. Cramer broke our unspoken agreement and directed his question at me.

"Tis better to be silent and be thought a fool,
than to speak and remove all doubt."

– ABRAHAM LINCOLN

I was young, sensitive, and acutely aware of what strangers took from their first impressions of me. I'm not a mind-reader, but a look of surprise on peoples' faces when I spoke probably meant that they didn't think that I could. Or on the other end of the spectrum, sometimes I open my mouth and people take me for some kind of secret genius. As a very young adult, I told myself that I had enough on my plate, and it was not my job to change other people's perceptions of super sexy disabled women. But truthfully, I was terrified of saying something that would destroy any kind of remarkable illusion.

Yet, taking a permanent pledge of silence is no satisfactory way of life. One needn't speak to be heard, but sometimes, each of us has a duty to make our feelings, experiences, and ideas known somehow. With a disability, I have constant close interactions with and reliance upon my caregivers. Every action I take is an exercise in planning, communication, and teamwork.

There are endless ways to cultivate a strong voice early on in life. In high school, after-school activities offer students a taste of acting as elected presidents and council members. My voice was heard, starting at an early age, in my annual individualized education planning meetings. IEP meetings are super boring, but very necessary to evaluate progress toward achievement when there is a special need. They were my first chance to share—with all levels of the school's administration—my truth. It's vital to speak up with intention to impact the trajectory of our own lives. It's never too early to begin and hardly ever too late.

Abe Lincoln didn't strictly follow his own advice. But if he hadn't broken his silence, the presidency would have eluded him, and the United States would not resemble what it is today. We are all born to make our mark on this world. If you have a voice, then do the world a favor and share it. There is undoubtedly a unique tone to what you have to offer. My voice is high-pitched, shaky, and cracks frequently. Like Elmo on steroids. But it gets the job done. If Mr. Cramer asked me the same question today, I would respond with what I believe: That it's important to move past barriers that are imposed on all of us based on strict ideas of sex and gender. The Anna of then was not yet ready. It took a long time for me to understand the potency of my own voice and how it can best be used. As it turns out, breaking the silence was the only way to begin.

*To the world you may be one person, but
to one person, you may be the world.*

—DR. SEUSS

ANNIE

There once was an amazing woman named Annie. I met her at muscular dystrophy summer camp when I was 19 years old and she was 20. Very quickly, she became important to me—for more than her smarts, confidence, style, unapologetic boldness, and the fact that she had been born with the same muscle disease as me.

Annie was the first person with a disability I had ever known in real life who not only set high expectations for herself but also blew passed them. When we met, I was in a period of waiting and planning as I slowly plugged away at community college courses. I was constructing an uncertain vision of living on my own and having a career I'd find meaningful. At the same time, Annie was doing just that.

Right after high school, Annie moved away from home to attend the University of Illinois at Urbana-Champaign. She completed her bachelor's degree in a mystifying three years and moved to Chicago for graduate school that fall. Annie earned her master's degree and continued on as a doctoral candidate, declaring that she would eventually become the leading disability sexuality researcher. In the middle of it all, she even started 3E Love, a company offering apparel and other merchandise that promotes disability acceptance and inclusion.

There was a time while she was at grad school that I was in the city and able to visit her and see her downtown apartment, a pretty impressive first floor place. Even as a poor grad student, Annie always demonstrated an image of a thriving woman in charge, giving everything she touched a very cool edge. The chance to see her in her apartment—with funky purple walls in every room and artwork to match her punk rock tattoos— offered a glimpse into what would be needed for me to achieve a similar independent lifestyle. That day gave texture to my dreams and showed me exactly what would be required if I were going to live on my own in a big city. In a word, it was grit.

Annie had a slight cold when I was there and I remember being concerned knowing how critical a common cold usually is for me and that she was going to be all alone when I left. She assured me that someone would be stopping by, probably a couple hours later, shrugging off the fragile nature of the loosely structured support system she depended on for so much—friends and paid caregivers who would come in periodically to assist her throughout the day. That's when I learned how to live with a disability and make strides ahead. It's like being an expert trapeze artist—you have to have killer instincts and know just the right moment to take a leap.

Less than a year after my visit, Annie's life of achievement, that ascending success story I was so emotionally tied to, came to a screeching halt. On January 20, 2009, much of the nation was celebrating the first inauguration of President Obama with feelings of hope for a brighter tomorrow thick in the air. That same day, I learned the devastating news that Annie had died from complications of a routine surgical procedure.

In only three years of watching how she lived her life, chatting with her at camp and get togethers, I learned countless invaluable lessons from Annie. She did not dream. She did not hesitate or wince at her goals. Annie demanded that her vision for herself come to fruition.

Annie first crossed my path at a time when I desperately needed to be reminded of the legitimacy of my dreams. We weren't close friends—more like acquaintances with many mutual connections. She wasn't a mentor or an icon. But Annie was my idol, marking the standard by which I measured my own future. She was the first person who made me feel like I could do anything I wanted with my life.

Annie is an important part of my past, and she is an even more significant part of my present. When things feel dark and the structures that are supposed to support me seem to be caving in on me, I think of Annie and her determination to live on her own terms. I consider how many people are out there crediting her for inspiring them in some way, taking action because of her example. Although Annie's journey was a short one, her work to change the way people view life with a disability will never die.

> 66

Do you know why we have the sunflowers? It's not because Vincent van Gogh suffered. It's because Vincent van Gogh had a brother who loved him. Through all the pain, he had a tether, a connection to the world. And that is the focus of the story we need – connection.

—HANNAH GADSBY

ISLAND LIFE

"No man is an island." This quote from English poet John Donne carries a truth I sometimes find too heavy to fully absorb. As a young girl, my mom often recited these words with a glance in my direction. She did her best to help me understand the illogical sense in striving for social isolation as a means to survival. It's counterproductive at the best of times and, I've learned, nonsensical during difficult times.

I've observed myself and others taking on all challenges alone when conquering challenge is all we know. Considering my commitment to live a great life rather than a mundane existence, at times it's felt like the universe was presenting me with an extra dose of adversity every step of the way. Setting a high personal standard of greatness is absolutely the consequence of having a great mother who can most accurately be described as my best advantage in life. By chance, she got her degree in special education before starting a family, and taught my brother and I from home whenever we weren't able to be physically present at school. She's a doer, an action taker. And her children, regardless of disabilities, were going to go to college and use their gifts to contribute to society if she had anything to do with it. And she did. Growing up, my mom showed me what hard work looked like. It was always clear that she believed in me. While I was in school, my mom was the best public relations representative money couldn't buy. She was also my teacher, my ambassador to the world, and sometimes my warrior.

For my entire upbringing, I was acquainted with the importance of sharing the ups and downs of life with others around me. Several times, people from my extended family, hometown, and beyond demonstrated clear devotion to the goodness of my mother. They stepped in to fill a need for me and my brother, surely because they knew my mother would do the same for any of them. The perfect example of this is when my brother and I were enrolled in community college. I was about 20 when my family's trusty, rusty, full-sized van came to the end of its road during the spring semester. Our beloved Ford Econoline was new in the mid-1980s, about the same time I was also brand-spanking-new to this crazy world.

We came to terms with the loss of transportation for me, my brother, and our motorized wheelchairs. Then, my mother quickly got about the business of figuring out how to get to and from our classes for the rest of that week. Due to the significant commute from our house to campus, we strategically chose classes on Tuesdays and Thursdays to condense our trips and save gas.

That's when we started to think about things in terms of Life Before—when we had a van and the ability to make deliberate decisions about how many trips we would take—and Life After—when we would need to borrow a van twice a week. My mom called anyone living within a 10-mile radius of our house whom she'd seen driving a full-sized van. Suddenly we were on constant lookout, like a search party on a very specific mission. How were we going to get to classes that week? Sometimes, my mom would approach complete strangers and tell them the tale of her ambitious young adult children and their need to achieve. She gave them her phone number and asked them to consider lending their vehicle for a day or two.

Several friends and acquaintances regularly approved our request. Each time, the routine was always the same; we cleared the back of the van, leaving empty space behind the front two seats. Our chairs were wheeled in the side door via our metal collapsible ramp. One at a time, my mom and a caregiver would lift my brother and me from our chairs onto a board with a cushion on it and slide us into the back of the van like two loaves of bread. Since these vans were not modified for the intended purpose of hauling around two disabled people and their wheelchairs in a safe manner, our 300-pound wheelchairs weren't secured to anything, at all. So, we decided that it was safer somehow that we not ride in them, opting for the wheelchairs to bounce freely as we laid unrestrained on the floor right next to them.

This situation was unsustainable for the long-term and eventually came to its natural end. One day, deep into the semester, we returned a van to our good family friends—following a minor, but unfortunate, fender bender on the way back from school. With a loving embrace, the couple told my mom they were so glad that everyone was okay after the accident. And then they informed us we were no longer welcome to borrow their van. A few days later, half of that same dear couple called. She and some of my mom's other friends wanted to organize a fundraiser so that we could have our own brand-new van.

After two months of planning, they held the fundraiser in the gym of the local middle school. Leading up to it, we were featured in the local TV news. A newspaper reporter even followed us around for a day as part of the publicity for the event. One of our community college instructors heard our story, sharing with all of her classes that we'd be at Northern Illinois University that fall and were seeking out new caregivers there to join our team. A future Huskie heard about this cool brother and sister duo and reached out. From that explosion of kindness, my family not only ended up with a reliable—and safer—form of transportation, but also a valuable friend who's still a member of my brother's team nearly 15 years later.

I've been fortunate in so many ways. Yet, being the recipient of so much kindness can be difficult to accept. When I moved away from home, I was resolved in my determination to become my own public relations representative, ambassador, and warrior. My mother will always be my teacher, and over time, I have come to understand the meaning behind her words, "No man is an island." There's value in the connection that grows when we share our needs with another person. Perhaps every one of us is like an island—independent and isolated at first glance, but inextricably linked, deep below the surface.

"

Life's most persistent and urgent question is:
What are you doing for others?

—MARTIN LUTHER KING, JR.

AN ED-UCATION

———

E very so often, an individual shows the world possibilities that can only be discovered through a life outside of the norm. Ed Roberts arrived at the perfect moment. Coming of age in the 1960s against a backdrop of open rage as a generation of youth demanded that society make some big changes. They longed for greater compassion. Roberts was poised to highlight an injustice that many people in the United States didn't even know existed. An oppressive barrier is no match for a positive attitude, especially when such a force is sustained by singular persistence to surpass it. Disability rights activist Ed Roberts' legacy, for me, is a prime example of this. With a presence of pure positivity and light, he made a lasting impact that no one could have anticipated.

Spanning from 1939 to 1995, Roberts' life offers a lesson to everyone. At age 14, he contracted polio—just one year before a vaccine became available. When he finally returned home from the hospital 18 months later, Roberts was paralyzed from the neck down and required a ventilator to breathe. The popular ventilator at the time was called an iron lung, a device where a person would lay inside of what looked a lot like a giant capsule with an airtight seal that encased their entire body up to the neck. The machine used negative air pressure to force the chest to expand at a set rate, provoking inhalation. Exhalation naturally followed. Many years later, in a *60 Minutes* interview, Roberts' mother recounted her sigh of relief when she realized that her son would survive polio. Her delight was met with a doctor's disgust. "What do you mean you're glad he's going to live? How would you like to live your life inside of an iron lung?"

Over time, Roberts broke free from the iron lung and began breathing with a ventilator attached to his motorized wheelchair. In yet another monumental achievement, he learned to operate the chair with the two fingers on his left hand that retained mobility. When he returned home from the hospital, Ed started out by participating in school over the phone. It didn't take long for his mother to insist that he attend school alongside his peers for a few hours, one day a week. Inch by inch, Roberts' world was expanding. In the classroom, Ed faced his deep fear of receiving attention because of his wheelchair. Roberts' feelings about the onlookers shifted at some point. He explained many years later that all of the gazes made him feel "like a star."

Eventually, Roberts applied to the University of California, Berkeley. Legend has it that when a dean on the acceptance committee learned of his severe disability, he insisted, "We've tried cripples before and it didn't work." Other staff disagreed. Roberts was ultimately admitted, making him the first student on campus with a severe physical disability. During his time at UC-Berkeley, Roberts earned both a bachelor's and a master's degree in political science, as he flourished as an advocate for himself and for others in the disability community. Using federal grant money, Roberts and some friends formed the Physically Disabled Students Program (PDSP). It was the first student organization on a college campus to focus on representation of students with disabilities.

Roberts joined the workforce in 1966 when he accepted a teaching position at a nearby community college. Not long after that, he was asked to take over as Executive Director for the Berkeley Center for Independent Living, the very first independent living center. According to my most recent Google search, Centers for Independent Living have reached more than four hundred locations worldwide.

Three years later, the governor of California appointed Roberts to run the state's Division of Vocational Rehabilitation. This was the same agency that, 14 years earlier, had refused services to Roberts, determining that he was "too disabled to work." In 1983, Roberts collaborated with other activists, including disability rights legend Judy Heumann, to establish the World Institute on Disability, a think-tank in Oakland, California devoted to the civil rights of people with disabilities. Heumann made many additional contributions of her own to the disability rights movement and eventually served as the first U.S. State Department Special Advisor on Disability Rights, under President Obama.

Roberts' life did not start out as a remarkable one. His youthful potential seemed to fade when polio took over his body, pushing him into a whole new way of existence. As disability became a part of Roberts' reality, it presented him with the decision to live or to surrender. Seeing Roberts' dependence on his wheelchair and ventilator, experts concluded that his future was bleak, with no possibility for joy or meaning in his life. Roberts understood that these were merely others' perceptions of his life. Once he decided to face the uncertainty, embrace the enhanced vulnerability that had become part of his every day, and move forward anyway, the negativity of others washed away. No longer could their dreary forecasting make an imprint on the way Roberts saw himself. He was left just as he was: perfectly whole.

Ed Roberts was among the first activists to share a story of optimism for life with a disability and share it loudly. His work helped set the standard in the disability rights movement of the 1960s. He and other advocates of the time declared that individuals with disabilities should have authority over their own lives, be active in their communities, and use their skills to contribute to the workforce. He left a lasting mark on everything he touched. Roberts' motorized wheelchair is now part of the permanent collection of the Smithsonian Institution, serving as a reminder of the person who drove it to such great heights, shining a bright light on society's limited way of thinking.

66

*Energy and persistence
conquer all things.*

—BENJAMIN FRANKLIN

UNIVERSAL
TRUTH

A gainst a backdrop of 100 billion stars in a universe of ten tril-
lion galaxies, I feel the wind of over seven billion people moving around me. With all of this activity, it can be a challenge to
pinpoint what really matters. But discovering what it is that you
truly value and putting all of your energy into it — whether that's
a person, a cause, an organization, or whatever you determine is
worthy of your personal passion — is the most fulfilling path.

While life on this planet presents what can seem like limitless possibilities for most people, those with disabilities have little
choice in where we live and what kind of work and activities fill
our days. Around us, everyone is busy working on the promise of
life, liberty, and the pursuit of happiness. Meanwhile, the disability
community is often consumed with trying to simply maintain *life*.
Yet, we see our nondisabled peers making strides towards self-ac-
tualization and professional achievement. Even when our minds
and bodies hold together long enough to reach our fullest potential, our support system can be yanked away without a whisper of

warning, leaving those of us who depend on government services scrambling to find new ways of having our basic needs met.

Around the time I relocated to Wisconsin, the state's newly instated Gov. Scott Walker was causing major controversy. Large crowds demonstrated in the streets and filled the capitol building after Walker severely reduced the collective bargaining rights of most state and municipal employees, including teachers. I was practically hit in the face with the passion of Wisconsinites right away.

There's an infectious spirit in the air in Wisconsin. People are enthusiastic about where they live and passionate about making sure their voices are heard by elected officials. It's nothing like my Illinois hometown, far from the capitol of Springfield, where few people were excited or even interested in civic engagement. Many had a blasé attitude towards voting and interacting with public servants. Perhaps it came from a repeated cycle of corruption at every level of government. Government felt like a distant entity until I arrived in Madison. Years later, when my independence was threatened, I felt the ripple effects of vocal, organized engagement all around me.

In 2016, Wisconsin Department of Health Services was trying to save taxpayer money. The proposed savings came from a reduction in disability support programs, like in-home caregiving and transportation services. These programs support many people with disabilities—including yours truly—so we can live safely in our homes and be active participants in the community.

In true Wisconsin fashion, disability-service professionals got to work to take action, making projections about how the cuts would affect those with disabilities and their families. Over the next few months, disability advocates from across the state united. DHS held listening sessions in response to gather information.

Then, the announcement. After a year and a half of organizing, issuing press releases, and engaging in media interviews, DHS released a statement saying they decided to postpone all proposed changes. With that, people with disabilities and our allies all over the state let out a huge sigh of relief. A simple press release restored confidence in the value of our collective voices. Suddenly, I felt hope that future budget discussions would consider those who would be impacted: we the people.

In that moment, I had a brief flash of clarity. Within the immensity that surrounds us, the unending noise that can feel so oppressive—the smallness I sometimes feel is merely an illusion. I can't say if someone is always listening, but I know that I'm never alone. Finding what you value is important in this life. Through the experience of activism, I will never again take for granted the services that make my life possible. As the years go by, I've realized more and more that supporting my values can only happen when working in unison with my friends and allies.

Just like Earth's 500 quadrillion grains of sand, uniting as one with others is the way to shape the tides.

"

A successful man is one who can lay a firm foundation with bricks others have thrown at him.

—DAVID BRINKLEY

BOUNCE

So many experiences teach us how to make a springboard out of a brick wall.

This morning, I woke up to a series of text messages from one of the most loyal and trusted members of Team Anna. We will call her Jasmine. Jasmine said, "I'm having a crisis, I can't come in tonight, I hope your mom will be there to take care of you."

I often face moments like this. I can't walk and I'm not able to move my arms, which means I'm quite dependent on:

1) Technology
2) The people around me

... Both of which are less than predictable.

My relationship with technology is a challenging one. I'm fortunate to have a machine that helps me breathe while I'm sleeping and a fancy chair that gets me where I need to go. But when one of these devices has a 'crisis,' I'm ill-equipped to handle it. One time in grad school, I had to brave a heavy, wet snow fall in downtown

Madison to make it to the required weekly seminar. Snow is usually no match for my motorized chair, but this time, enough moisture seeped into the computer system to send me spinning around uncontrollably. In this instance, my areas of expertise weren't useful. I couldn't reason with the chair. I couldn't talk through its issues or negotiate until we came to a mutual understanding. So, I resorted to empty threats of violence.

With people, I have a better rapport. Many folks have made their way through my rotation of caregivers and, over time, I have slowly developed a solid system of support. It's been a learning process. I now know that even the most dependable people have moments of crisis, illness, family drama, car issues, etc. Any of these unexpected elements can cause a hiccup in my day. If the caregiver is willing, we can discuss the problem. And, in that scenario, we can almost always come up with a good solution together. Cooperation is critical if you want to cultivate a solid foundation in teamwork, as well as gain personal confidence through leadership.

And by the end of a good discussion, my caregiver and I can typically come to understand each other's needs better. Because truly, we take care of one another. It goes both ways. Balance is key for any operation to be successful, even – perhaps especially – with the dynamic between a caregiver and the recipient of that care.

When it is time to take a step forward—apply for a new job, buy a house, launch a business, start a family—we all need the help of others. Love and support needs to be behind us in every significant endeavor. Even when the people in your life seem to be causing complications, I am certain you are getting something out of the experience that will help you become a better you.

Jumping back to the present circumstance, it seems that Jasmine and I are due for a good conversation. In the meantime, I took advantage of the evening alone to devote some much needed time on projects I'd been neglecting ... and I wrote this essay.

66

To be yourself in a world that is
constantly trying to change you is the
greatest accomplishment.

—RALPH WALDO EMERSON

TRICK-OR-TREAT

You might think that dress-up is for kids, but there are many of us who rely on costumes well into adulthood. I have always been a dreamer. When I was a little girl, I didn't need a special occasion to become anything or anyone I wanted. I would regularly borrow my friend's dance recital costumes, which were always adorned in sequins, just to lay around my house wearing tap shoes. Then there was my Little Mermaid phase ...

Now that I'm a 'grown-up,' my friends and I still play dress-up. But these days, it's not always to stand out. Instead of creating an appearance that reflects who we truly are or want to become, it's tempting to use our wardrobes as camouflage. Often without realizing it, we use fashion trickery as a civilized defense mechanism—a way of distracting onlookers from whatever truth we're frightened to disclose about ourselves.

I've had to abandon the possibility of hiding the truth. Everything that's truly vulnerable about me is on permanent display. I sit in a motorized wheelchair with an obvious lack of muscle mass in my arms and legs. When people meet me, they think they understand me deeply. But they don't know me at all. That tiny amount of personal information provided by my physical appearance often leads strangers to immediately think that they know my capabilities and what my life must be like. What's worse, some people think that there is nothing more to know than my physical characteristics.

So, it's a challenge for me to make an authentic first impression. I'm especially sensitive to my obvious vulnerability at certain times and places. When I approach the receptionist upon arriving at a job interview, there are many questions likely running through their head.

Can she do the job?
Will she be reliable?
How will she be able to work in a team environment?
What if she gets sick?
Is she sick right now?

By design, I'm looking very put together in these instances. This can catch people—the ones who think they know what it must be like to have a disability—off guard. For some reason, wearing makeup and professional clothing makes other people treat you like a real human being. Any way that I can remind people that my life is about more than my desire to survive is important. My intention for each day is all about thriving, and people should see that.

I choose to live openly and honestly. From hair and makeup to my carefully-selected outfits – perhaps a cardigan with jeans or maybe a romper, but these days, only if it's 20 degrees out and I can defy some reasonable conventionality like Ways to Avoid Hypothermia – I have a duty to myself to always express the true me.

I am clear about who I am and what I want. I don't shy away from questions. Accepting myself helps me relate better to others; creating the interpersonal connections that supports our individual evolution. When you live authentically, what you get in return is pretty sweet.

66

We are all in the gutter, but some of
us are looking at the stars.

—OSCAR WILDE

A MESSAGE
WORTH CONVEYING

———

"How do you stay so positive?" she asked, looking at me with sparkling blue eyes.

The question made me quite nervous. I've never thought of myself as having a very sunny disposition. But I certainly didn't want to stomp all over the untarnished optimism beaming from my new caregiver. Each day, I generally hope for the best while preparing for the worst.

I thought carefully before responding. It was a valid question. Most of my muscles don't work much, if at all. In order to survive, I require caregivers like the one who was standing before me. To live on my own terms, I must verbalize my needs and communicate my plans effectively to caregivers. There are no solo activities. I am a collaborator in every aspect of my life.

Caregivers support the special attention that must be paid to all parts of my body. I tend to sit or lay in one place for longer periods of time than most people do. Although I have full sensation everywhere in my body and can detect discomfort instantly, I must be intentional about having someone move me around or reposition me fairly frequently. Otherwise, pressure sores can form on my skin from the weight of my body. If they occur, such wounds can take a very long time to heal. Stiffness further limits my ability to move, so I must monitor circulation in my arms and legs and stretch them regularly. Lack of muscle strength diminishes how much my lungs can expand. Doctors have instructed me to use special equipment to exercise them and clear any junk out, giving extra tender love and care to the ol' breathers.

This daily body care adds up to a lot of time in my routine—all directed by me and carried out by others. Some days, I think that my life amounts to running through the same schedule. Yet, everything I do serves its purpose. Each check mark on my tedious task list is in perfect alignment with my intention to reach larger accomplishments. At times, it feels as though I'm riding a conveyor belt. While I am the one making the judgment calls on how I spend my time, I'd be lying if I said I don't often feel like a passenger on this ride, a routine that leaves little room for spontaneity. Skipping one step means experiencing a negative side effect later, potentially triggering a downward spiral that completely derails me from course. It takes four hours for my caregivers and me to complete the basic life-supporting activities that mean I'm ready for the day. It's also about four hours of routine before we can close the curtain on that same day. This is my reality.

Which brings me back to that question in question: How do I stay so positive? Looking at my new caregiver's hopeful face, I saw no sense in worrying about trivial labels like *optimism* or *pessimism*. I don't like labels anyway. There are certain things we can't change about our lives. We must make deliberate choices to make the most of what we can, while we can.

In this time of social media and other digital dependencies, we tell ourselves that we're more connected than ever. In truth, our society keeps finding new and inventive ways of sanitizing and digitizing the messiness out of our daily lives. The amount of research and data we have available at our fingertips is endless. We can find out anything at any time. There are sources and platforms for voices with every point of view, making it ever more possible to live in separate silos of communication and information. Even our disagreements are ever more taking place where we can log off at any time.

This, I suppose, is what makes me a bit of a unicorn these days. Editing certain people and perspectives out of my existence is not an option. I deeply depend on a lot of people from many different backgrounds. My life requires that I live with an open mind and an open heart, and my interactions are up-close and personal every day. What happens after someone new enters my space is impossible to predict. I've experienced incredible rewards and heartbreaking negative consequences as a result of my innate vulnerability. My unique experience sets me up for life-changing, valuable relationships. Interactions with my caregivers, individuals with whom I wouldn't otherwise encounter, illuminate and expand my life far beyond what I could have imagined for myself.

Just like anyone who has ever lived, I get up in the morning knowing there is potential for some good, a little bad, and maybe some ugly. I have to have a somewhat rigid daily routine and I have to pay extra attention to detail for the sake of my health. So what? Because I must rely on others for my care, I have to open myself up to the unpredictability of interacting with other fallible humans. No matter how I'm feeling about my life on any given day, this openness builds a strength in me that is priceless.

Cripes, maybe I am an optimist after all.

There is no need to reach for the stars.
They are already within you -
just reach deep into yourself.

—UNKNOWN

SUPER POWERFUL

Being a superhero would be cool for a lot of reasons. My favorite is wearing outrageous outfits in public (often including tights!) while maintaining everyone's respect. Unfortunately, this is not that kind of world—one where accidents cause supernatural capabilities and the hero always wins a battle against the evil villain. But this is the real world, which I am not the best fit for.

My life is *complicated*. Because of my disability, I need other people to help me do almost everything. This is where The Team comes in. These amazing people assist me first thing in the morning and throughout my day: getting out of bed and into my chair, to the bathroom, combing my hair, washing my face, dressing, a breathing treatment (when I'm feeling like a super responsible adult), your typical 10-step makeup routine, and then getting me secured into the passenger side of my van and driving me to meetings and appointments. They literally support me. I trust each team member with my life every day. That's because all members of Team Anna are interviewed, hired, trained, and scheduled by me. My day-to-day life resembles what I imagine it would be like to run a large corporation. Except that my role offers no time off, paid or otherwise. And my life depends on everyone doing their part, executing their responsibilities in a thoughtful and conscientious manner.

Daily life looks like a breeze for many people in our era of high-speed technology, instant results, and so many handy gadgets (thanks to Steve Jobs and all of the other Silicon Valley college dropouts). The answer to 'Can we have it all?' seems to be a resounding 'Yes!' for the rest of the world. But for me, it's a little bit different. With a disability, so much of my time is filled with recruiting, training, and scheduling staff—in addition to maintaining the documentation required for publicly funded support services. It leaves me constantly colliding with a different question. Where does someone like me find the time and energy for a career that makes a meaningful impact on the world?

"No life ever grows great until it is focused, dedicated, and disciplined," according to a Harry Emerson Fosdick quote I came across in high school. I had it written out and posted on my bedroom wall as a regular reminder to strictly spend time on things that would allow me to move closer to my goals. As I've gotten older, this code has become harder and harder to live by. If, like me, you are living on planet Earth, then we have a few things in common.

1. We only get 24 hours per day.
2. The demands of each passing minute can feel endless.

If you are even more like me, your personal expectation to always be accomplishing more translates into a recurring dizzy spell as you try to distinguish essential tasks from nonessential ones.

For instance, many times I've skipped my daily breathing treatment and spent the extra time on something that seemed more pressing. Like working for my employer late into the night, adding an early meeting the next day with one of the human service agencies that provides me support, or coordinating unexpected details of my caregiver schedule for the week. Consistent demands like these can squeeze my routine tighter and tighter.

But not giving my lungs the attention they require has its consequences. Serious ones. Consequences that can throw off my plans in life for at least several weeks of illness—a period of time that requires I stick to a rigorous routine of exhausting breathing treatments every two or three hours. Each treatment while fighting a cold involves a variety of aggressive medical devices—one in particular that helps force air into my lungs and pull junk out. That stretch of illness is followed by a difficult recovery as my body gets back to its normal strength and endurance, where I can breathe on my own and live my life as I normally do. In my first year navigating life as an employed adult living on my own, I had three severe respiratory infections in 12 months—a record for me. Afterwards, I decided to bump my lungs up on the priority list. Giving my lungs a little time and attention with a single 20-minute treatment each day is a small price compared to the avalanche of struggle that can occur when I allow my health to get off balance. Maybe I can't do everything or 'have it all.' But I also can't have a fulfilling career without breathing.

I'm on the other side of that seemingly ridiculous yet profound revelation; I'm taking each day as it comes and trying to make good choices along the way. We all must make occasional compromises to move forward with our goals. Progress takes time. Perhaps there's no perfect formula for achieving a great life. It may feel limiting at times, but this segment of the multiverse offers many grand possibilities to each of us. Sometimes, you can be your own villain, but you can also be your own hero.

66

It is a terrible thing to see and have no vision.
We would never learn to be brave and patient
if there were only joy in the world.

—HELEN KELLER

TRUST

Naked and Afraid isn't just a reality show—it's basically me on any given day. Even when I'm fully clothed and in the privacy of my own home, everything I do is on full display to the people I rely on daily. Because my muscles are weak, I come strong in numbers everywhere I go. In no aspect of my day, from bathing, dressing, eating, watching Netflix, going to the bar, going to work, going number one and number two—am I without company. Not only that, but my home is their workplace. Sometimes they vent about life. Sometimes they decide to tell me that they can't cover a shift as I'm about to nod off to sleep. Yet, I've collected a solid group of caregivers who literally support me. Over time, many of them have become trusted allies. I depend on them for my survival and, many times, friendship and counsel.

But recently, I discovered that a significant amount of my humble earnings was missing from my wallet. A vigorous search made it impossible to ignore the truth—one of my trusted allies took the cash. I felt violated.

Several years ago, I moved to Madison, Wisconsin. I had all kinds of hesitations as I broke out of my familiar, small-town life in Illinois. It was my first time living away from my family. After several independent study projects on domestic violence towards women with disabilities, I was acutely aware of my high risk for abuse and being taken advantage of. But a sense of desperation to lead a life defined in all ways by me won out over fear.

Seemingly meaningless, trivial decisions create depth and form the true life of an individual. You know, like eating ice cream for breakfast and cereal for dinner, wearing just my underwear for pajamas (without a thought as to what my mom would say), sleeping in all morning, or not going to sleep at all and streaming classics like the third season of *Grey's Anatomy*. Without the ability to make choices that shape our days—outside of survival, work, and social interactions—there's no room for moments of unexpected inspiration or passion. A life of such freedom is the ultimate privilege. To achieve it, I would have to leave behind the shell of protection inherent in being surrounded by a loving family.

I've always had an active imagination. It's gotten the best of me in times of worry. Each new person I invite into my world, my home, my sanctuary, is a new element of the unknown. Will he or she be exactly who they say? Or, is there a sinister side that I don't yet see? These questions lurk in the back of my mind as I onboard every new caregiver. At best, a horrifying new hire would make lots of suggestions on the first day about my routine ("How did you come up with your combination of daily supplements, Anna? I have some ideas ..."). At worst, that friendly face could disguise a predator who can't resist the impulse to smother me with a pillow in my sleep. When my mind starts down that dark and thorny road, trading in a shell of protection for a gang of strangers seems utterly idiotic. I knew it would only take a single calloused soul to inflict major damage upon my sense of safety. Distinguishing procedures of wise caution from paranoia is a game that I have not mastered.

But running with worst-case scenarios exclude the best possibilities. In reality, outside of my exhaustive imagination, I've seen the goodness in people. In the several years since I became a Madisonian, I've created countless memories with the people I've recruited, trained, and welcomed into my life. I've shared my many victories with some very special people. To do this, I've stared uncertainty in the face. I've learned a lot about myself and my gut. I now know how to follow my instincts and effectively handle difficult situations.

My time in Madison has afforded me huge opportunities and countless adventures. So, I got a little robbed. I had a hole poked in my trust and obliviousness. But I gained so much more. I know what to do when people in my life want to harm me—never back down. I won't be discouraged from pursuing a life of riches for fear of what craziness might come. The real crime would be shying away from the high expectations I have for my life.

I consider myself a lucky woman for many reasons. Following this unfortunate theft, I see that the amazing experiences and people I have known up to this point have come into my life in a beautiful configuration. I see much more than coincidence around me. Living a full life with a disability requires that I be open and vulnerable for whatever comes my way. The truth about my missing cash will eventually come out. Until then, I'll follow the advice printed on the currency that was taken from me: In God We Trust.

*If human beings are perceived as potentials
rather than problems, as possessing strengths
instead of weaknesses, as unlimited rather
than dull and unresponsive, then they thrive
and grow to their capabilities.*

—BARBARA BUSH

TRUE LOVE REQUIRES NO LUCK AT ALL

Finding your dream job is as rare as finding true love ... but less rare than unicorns. The path to discovering each of these—okay, maybe minus the unicorns—is a similarly confusing, zigzagging journey.

When it comes to finding the right match in love, as well as in employment, I'm a believer. Heartache and heartbreak surface in each pursuit. But pain and disappointment are necessary companions when deciding what you want and pursuing it. To follow your dreams, you have to regularly expose your strengths and vulnerabilities.

The time I remember falling out of love was with my first job. As a newly minted rehabilitation counselor, I entered the workforce with vigor and optimism. My field was a direct reflection of my own background and experiences—a profession dedicated to assisting people with disabilities in navigating challenges, addressing ambivalence, and pursuing professional goals. My excitement at the beginning of the job search gradually deflated over the 15 months it took me to secure employment. When it happened, I was extremely grateful for my own office and a new place to call home—alongside some of the most esteemed professionals in my local area. I had a great working relationship with my direct supervisor. We met at least weekly to touch base about my clients and ensure that we were on the same page.

But a year in, new upper management entered the picture. They implemented changes, putting the previously quaint non-profit organization under the strict protocols characteristic of a regimented corporation. Employees now had to document each of their activities for every hour of the work day and name the program or service that said activities fell under. The minute I heard this announcement, I knew that it was bad news for me.

I can't work the way others do. I operate the computer with the assistance of another person or some nifty software, like Dragon NaturallySpeaking, which allows me to speak into a microphone to control the cursor and dictate notes for documentation. At all times and in every setting, it takes me more time to accomplish a task. Eating a snack, taking a drink, adjusting my position in my chair—each of these regular biological necessities interrupt my productivity. If I had to pee while I was at the office, I had to take my work home with me. There was a pristine and expansive wheelchair-accessible stall in the restroom at work, however, I was never able to make use of that lovely facility since it didn't have a motorized lift to transfer me from my wheelchair to the toilet. I never had the guts to share this detail with my bosses, which added to the complexity of me trying to help others understand how I navigate my work practices. Matching the performance time of my colleagues was never going to happen, but I never failed to meet a deadline. I was originally elated when the executive director approved my request to double my hours. My direct supervisor and I were preparing to unveil a new client service. I knew it would be a while before I built a caseload to fill the additional time, but everything seemed to be falling into place rather naturally. My enthusiasm to take on more work turned to horror as the new time-logging policy was introduced, ensuring that my work time was about to be under increased scrutiny.

Typically a good challenge is my playground, but this was a big one. In fact, the program we were rolling out was meant to assist people with physical disabilities in moving forward personally and professionally. My supervisor and I developed a plan of outreach. We shared our offerings with local entities that served our target demographic. All of the evidence we had made it clear that, at least the employment part would make for a tough program to sell—regardless of it being free of charge to individuals. My eyes were wide open to the barriers of people with disabilities in the workplace.

Few of the people with disabilities I know have gainful employment. According to a report published by the U.S. Department of Labor in 2019, 19.3% of people with disabilities were employed, compared to 66.3% of people without disabilities. Many factors contribute to this. To start, the first illustrations of what living with a disability is like—quality of life, potential for achievement, and any kind of satisfaction in this world, etc.—largely rests in the hands of doctors. These doctors are often the ones who relay the news about the presence of disability. The way said doctors convey information about disability has a dramatic impact on their patients and doctors have a bad habit of painting the worst possible picture. If parents learn for the first time that their young child has a disability, then the doctor giving that information has a big responsibility not to diminish the potential for that child's future achievement with damaging words of a grim outlook. For parents of any child, it's much easier to stomach a slow and steady dose of low expectations than to see that look of heartbreak on their kid's face when, at some point, life serves up a disappointment. And the truth is, this world can be cruel. Employers, whether they realize it or not, close the door to opportunity for qualified candidates with disabilities far too often. For anyone seeking out a new job, having a gap in your employment history, for instance, makes it extra difficult to even get an interview. From my time in the field of rehabilitation counseling, I have seen how frequently changes in an individual's health and support system can cause disruptions to employment. And that's if someone is open to the possibility of working in the first place.

Through countless client conversations, I now have a better understanding of how rare it is for someone with a disability to pursue work. I can't tell you how many times a client shut down the topic of employment. Because for many people, the idea of working is too risky. Employment may mean putting their government benefits—a consistent Social Security check, government-funded caregivers, etc.— in jeopardy due to income restrictions for social safety net programs. My colleagues and I did a lot of work to educate about how one can engage in employment while receiving government benefits. But it was hard to convey confidence that the rules would always remain the same, and no surprises would pop up along the way. When you have a disability of any kind, you often have a close relationship with that stomach-churning feeling that comes when the rug is suddenly jerked out from under you. When that is your reality, you cling to stability wherever you can find it—I know I do. Whatever the cause, people with disabilities of every age have a lack of confidence related to the prospect of employment. This is a problem everywhere and it has existed since the beginning of time.

With the changes being incorporated at my job, it felt like my professional life was imploding around me. I called a meeting right away. Sitting at a conference room table with my caregiver, direct supervisor, and two members of upper management, I articulated my concerns around the new hourly documentation mandate and why it wasn't appropriate to measure my work with the same metric as my colleagues. They all listened intently. To the credit of the higher ups, they didn't want me to jeopardize my work-life balance. They were alarmed that I was routinely finishing my work at home after hours. They tossed around ideas about side projects to fill my increased number of hours until there were enough referrals to the new program to top off my caseload. But in the end, it was clear that any work completed outside the 8-hour work day would not be recognized.

Eventually, I got some projects that helped fill my time and show my contribution to the organization. But that supply of work dried up quickly. I was promptly questioned about the tasks in my weekly log. Various tactics were used to solve the growing question of "*What to do with Anna?*" I certainly didn't have the answer. I tried to tell them why their disability-focused organization should understand how my disability affects the way I conducted my work. The message was not getting through. Next, the director recommended doing an assessment to explore other technologies to help me work faster. Unfortunately, the assessment yielded no helpful discoveries.

This relationship was undeniably on the rocks. I felt sick as soon as I entered the building. When putting the final touches on each weekly timesheet, my anxiety multiplied by 11. After my first less-than-dazzling annual review, I knew it was time for me to go. During the last couple months leading up to that moment, I realized I only had one survival strategy left: hide. That is not a winning approach if you want to justify your paycheck by showing off all you have to offer. I submitted my notice just before leaving the office to go to the holiday party. As the celebration was happening around me, it was bittersweet to see so many warm faces that I had come to know as my equals. I could see many reasons to stay—one was my direct supervisor, who had always been a reliable mentor and advocate for my talents. I hated to believe it, but it was no longer a place I could call home.

It's assumed that people with disabilities will stay in the same job until they can no longer work, which is often the case. What's implied is that people with disabilities should be so grateful for any job that they wouldn't dare risk it to seek out a better one. I reject that. I knew I had to go back out into the dark, scary world to find a job that was right for me.

With so much on the line in this life of love and work, there's always the temptation to contort ourselves into a person we don't recognize—someone we believe will be appealing to others. In both love and employment, finding the right path brings moments that can be ruthless and unforgiving. That's how we come to really understand who we are. We sail these treacherous waters and make it to the other side. Even if we have a few wounds to show for it, we can be confident that the challenge helped us discover a strength we didn't know before.

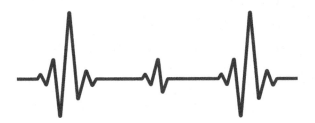

66

What lies behind us and what lies
before us are tiny matters compared to
what lies within us.

—RALPH WALDO EMERSON

DREAD AND DIRTY EXTRACTION

———

"You're in charge, Anna," he said. "We will follow your lead." He was the anesthesiologist who was about to assist with the extraction of my wisdom teeth. We will call him Dr. Dread.

I was 29 when I finally scheduled what was supposed to be a minor outpatient procedure. My family and I decided I should have it in the hospital as a safety precaution. The same doctors extracted my older brother's wisdom teeth several years before in the same hospital. Everything had gone smoothly for him. As the nurses wheeled me into the operating room, I was feeling confident and relaxed. The mood was light as I joked, talking with them about my tattoos. I asked if they liked their jobs and offered each of them a role on my team. Then, I drifted to sleep.

The next thing I remember was looking around the same room and seeing the same people around me. This time everything was blurry. My previous state of ease was suddenly knocked off kilter as I realized my breathing had become more strained.

Clearly and directly I said, "I can't breathe. You need to go get my mom. She's out in the waiting room."

I was in the hospital. Of course, I wanted my mommy –but the purpose behind my words went much deeper than that. If I told my mom I was having trouble breathing, she would know exactly what to do—immediately lower the head of the gurney so that whatever was in my lungs could start draining down and out. Through time and experience, my mom and I have developed reliable shorthand in addressing any complications I encounter with breathing. I knew I was surrounded by some well-trained and competent professionals. I also knew they would require more instruction than I could provide in the frantic state I found myself in.

One of the same soothing voices that had just gently declined my job offer responded to my instruction. "You're fine, honey." She set the oxygen mask on my face. I said, "No, no!" But she laid the mask over my nose and mouth anyway. This made me lose all sense of calm. I was overwhelmed with panic. The stupid disability that I have lived with my whole life prevents me from using my arms and legs. Communication is everything to me. In one casual motion, that nurse had blocked my one means of survival.

For reasons I couldn't explain, my breathing was getting worse by the second. I knew I was in trouble. What made me feel more desperate was knowing the people around me thought that I was confused about how much air was getting into my lungs. The numbers displayed on their fancy equipment were saying, "Everything's dandy with Anna." I needed to tell them the truth. I didn't know why, but my body was struggling.

I wiggled my nose and mouth, successfully causing the oxygen mask to shift off center, allowing me to speak.

"I need you to get my mom. I can't breathe," I said.

"You're fine. You're okay," the nurse replied. This time she secured the oxygen mask to my face, stretching the strap attached to it around the back of my head. That was it. It was too traumatic for me to bear. Only the horror in my widening eyes could express the terrible thing she had just done. My words were no longer there to support me. Game over. I fell back to sleep.

I woke up again. My vision was blurrier. I could feel thick fluid in my lungs. The mask was still over my face, but I fought through the fog, locking my eyes on one of the nurses. She noticed me as I was frantically raising my eyebrows up and down in an attempt to say, "Help!" After she removed my mask, I said "Please, you need to get my mom. I really can't breathe."

Again, the nurse assured me that everything was fine, and she placed the mask back on my face. Again, I said, "No!" Again, she ignored me. *What is wrong with these people?* I remember thinking. *Have I been abducted by aliens?* In that moment, it was hard to believe what I was experiencing. I couldn't think of another time where I was in the company of someone who completely understood my words but chose not to act on them. In this case, I was with a whole team of people who were charged with the task of protecting me. Somehow, listening to me did not seem to be part of it. I felt like I was in the Upside Down. I fell back to sleep.

This cycle continued several more times. Each time I was conscious, life was more and more foggy. All I could understand was that my breathing was getting worse and worse, and the people who were supposed to be caring for me didn't believe what I was saying.

Eventually, I woke up in a bed in a room with a TV on the wall and several comfy chairs—clearly a place meant for patients who needed to stay a while. My lips felt dry and stiff. I tried to form some words. What felt like about a million tiny cuts around my mouth made themselves known with a sensation that I can only compare to having a match lit on my face. Then I realized there was a tube down my throat to make me breathe. Several hours later, I was given a mirror. I saw dried blood in patches around my mouth and an empty space where one of my bottom front teeth had lived until I entered this enemy territory. I looked exactly like I felt—like I had been fighting in a battle all day.

But opening my eyes this time to see my family sitting around me was the most comforting feeling in the world. My mom, my dad and my brother—my most trusted allies. They know me and, most importantly, they listen to me.

When I looked at my brother, he said in the most spectacular sarcastic tone, "How was your day, Anna?"

In that moment, with the tube down my throat, laughing was not an option. So, I cried. Uncontrollably. I couldn't yet tell of the horror I had just endured—but my appreciation of sarcasm was back, my humor was back, things made sense again. Everything was going to be okay. I learned in the days that followed exactly how the plan to extract my wisdom teeth went so terribly wrong.

I was supposed to be in a twilight sedation throughout the procedure. Going in, we had agreed that, due to the limited extent I am able to open my mouth, the easiest way to help me breathe during the procedure would be to insert a tube up my nose, allowing the maximum amount of space for the endodontist to work. No one expected, including me, that my nose and nasal passages might be unusually small. Turns out, I had been accumulating 29-year-old problems with a child-sized nose. Even better. When Dr. Dread realized that he didn't have the right sized tube on hand to get me to sleep and secure my airway, he pushed forward. Literally. He continued to push the same device up my nose, moving from one nasal passageway to the other, for two full hours. Blood began to drain into my lungs, restricting my breathing.

As I explained what I was feeling, each desperate plea was ignored. Instead, my words and frantic eyebrow movements were interpreted as a need for more pain medicine. Dr. Dread pumped me with the potent pain drug fentanyl, the #1 possible side-effect being depression of the respiratory system. All of my distress exhibited the exact signs that he and his colleagues were trained to read as requests for more pain medication. These drugs further compromised my ability to breathe. Eventually, the machines alerted the medical team to the reality that I had been experiencing for hours: ANNA CAN'T BREATHE. By the time the professionals realized what was going on, it was too late for modest action. I needed air fast. It was time for intubation. To make room for a tube to go in my mouth and down my throat to force air in, they extracted one of my bottom front teeth.

The medical team didn't set out to put my life in danger that day. As extensively trained professionals, they used their knowledge and expertise, following protocols. All hospital policies were respected—but my wishes were not. This wasn't an incident with intention to harm. But the most difficult thing for me to process was the realization that no one had been considering me at all.

The tube stayed in for a day and a half. When I left the hospital, I was connected to a portable ventilator as I didn't yet have the strength to breathe on my own. From there, I went to the safest place on this planet: my mom's house. It was not a matter of when, but if my strength would return. If I was going to get back to my old self again, I would need to welcome my strength in my home, the place where I found it to begin with. Indeed, it came to me. My voice came back to me. Reasons to laugh came back to me. Everything that mattered returned, along with something new.

I spent two weeks recovering—an ugly process that consisted of building up my endurance to breathe on my own and healing my very sore throat and vocal cords. What I had been left with after my traumatic hospital experience equated to barely a hiss and a whisper rather than the human voice I had grown accustomed to beforehand. All the while, I was periodically spitting out chunks of dried blood that had filled my sinus cavity following Dread's repeated attempts to intubate through my nose. It felt much like an exorcism.

I did a lot of thinking over these couple of weeks. I thought about all the other times that I had been down before, pushed aside, disregarded, and ignored. I thought about a few times that a person or agency responsible for meeting my biological needs chose to silence me and my wishes rather than respecting my knowledge about what's best for me.

Then, I had a revelation about my place in this world. Each little cut and the wound that heals over it, all of these memories are gifts. Because I have this history, I'm aware of others who are being pushed aside, disregarded, and ignored. I know what it's like to be a powerful person without the tools to fight. I can see all of the other invisible people like me. For those of us who have had these experiences, it's up to us to help lift each other up.

66

You are responsible for your life. If you're sitting around waiting on somebody to save you, to fix you, to even help you, you are wasting your time. Only you have the power to move your life forward.

—OPRAH WINFREY

#NEVERSETTLE

―――――――

"Not Just Here for Your Viewing Pleasure." Sometimes I want to get T-shirts made with these words printed across my chest. I was on this planet for quite some time before I realized that some men find me attractive, somewhere in my mid-20s I would say. Before that, boys and a life of romantic antics were not explored by me nor was it encouraged by those around me. Never explicitly stated, but probably to protect my feelings from potential demolition, my closest allies in life showered me with a lot of, "Look over there, Anna ... There's achievement, success, and independence. Nothing to see over here." → [penis]

Don't get me wrong. I've been on the receiving end of some lovely flattery. But the invention of a trusty tool to pause and freeze-frame, would have helped me examine the occasional smile and side glance coming my way from a fellow. It would have blown wide open my narrow understanding that a man knew I was not only a human, but a female one.

Part of being fully human is acknowledging all that is uniquely special to the experience, and romance is often a big part of it.

For some reason, many people find it a bit absurd for someone with a disability to put themselves out there in the dating game. It's an arena with huge risks—but also great potential rewards. Much to my dismay, it's seen as novel for a disabled person to get married and have children. Most people grow up with the automatic assumption that they'll eventually find a partner and start a family. I make it a point not to believe in automatic assumptions. Everyone is different. Each of us should be able to achieve our own definition of a dream life. But the expectations of outsiders, whatever they may be, shouldn't be a factor. I've never felt like I was seen as good partner material. As a person with a disability, I've often gotten the vibe that I'm supposed to take my eggs and go sit in the corner while everyone else is partying on the dance floor.

I had an epiphany in college that maybe there's enough time for achievement, contribution to society *and* fun and exploration. Immediately, a mental shift began. Maybe there *was* someone worthwhile out there, even if he wasn't currently beating down my front door. It was time for something a little more daring. I created my first online dating profile, and from the flood of messages in my inbox, I realized quite suddenly how entirely wrong I had had it all along. It wasn't a case of me being so complex that no one would really 'get me.' Nor that no man would be able to find me attractive. As it turns out, the barricade to my love life was a simple cost-benefit analysis. For so many men over the years, a flicker of interest was no match for practical matters. Like concern over what other people would think. Or uncertainty about getting tangled up with someone living outside the norm. This very real and tangible way that others' perceptions were holding back my life felt like the worst kind of sick joke.

When I was finished feeling bad about my love life, I decided to ignite it. I agreed to go on some first dates with guys I had met online—a place where the public perception had no place. I met some interesting and lovely people. And my new dating life jumpstarted a routine of visiting my favorite bar once a week, just to meet new people who thought my jokes were funny. I learned to distinguish the nice guys from the guys who said nice things I wanted to hear. I figured out exactly how far openness and honesty could get me. Pushing these boundaries led me to more good times, as well as a fair amount of rejection. I encountered people and experiences that I wouldn't have known if I hadn't decided to push a little closer to the edge of my comfort zone. My bold and enthusiastic personality made me a magnet for a certain kind of man: artistic, sensitive, and often brooding in his own pain.

As soon as I developed an eye for spotting him, I found him around nearly every corner. Concealed by so many different faces, it always started off the same way. I excitedly learned about his unique creative style as I got a sense that nothing else in the world mattered other than our moments together. Meanwhile, he was completely mesmerized by everything I had to say. Then, after a while, the sparkle always faded, and the insecurities came out. He would push away from my expectations and concerns, saying that he didn't want to hurt me. But I knew every time that what he really meant was that he didn't want to 'ruin me.' As if that were possible. It's challenging for me to breathe under normal circumstances. Finding myself held up on such a high pedestal, the thin air and constant headache left me in a distinct kind of misery. That is when I would, on cue, end it with him or find some inventive way to fall from grace.

So, I turned the page from that stage, one in which I played around with boys who were drawn to me at first glance but wanted nothing to do with the messiness of my real life. I learned a lot from dating. My fashion and beauty routine will always be just for me, whether I am in a relationship or not. If living a big, satisfying life means moving outside of my comfort zone, then I'll be fearless in sharing all aspects of myself with someone I find special.

I'm content with who I am. I'm especially thankful that everything I need is already within me. Being on my own is not the same as being alone—or lonely. Someday, while I'm busy living my dreams, I may look over and find I'm with a worthy individual. One who dares to get close enough to go the distance with me, who accepts me as my whole human self. That would be one of many grand possible endings.

66

Many times we are our worst enemy. If we could learn to conquer ourselves, then we will have a much easier time overcoming the obstacles that are in front of us.

—STEPHAN LABOSSIERE

IF ONLY

There's a crack in my existence. The chasm between my reality and where I'm supposed to be—the life I believe that I can achieve—is deep and wide. What's keeping me from reaching the other side—where the contributions needed from me are waiting—are a couple of my oldest foes: time and doubt.

Like basically everyone in this world, I have essentials to tend to for health and hygiene. Then there's an additional never-ending laundry list of routine demands: job, bills, student loans, a dog with a high degree of self-esteem to accommodate, and invaluable relationships that I want to keep alive while I still am. Time has taught me that as my responsibilities grow greater, my days seem shorter. If time were a rubber band, my days would be stretched so tight that they lose their elasticity. With that, they lose all prospect of spontaneity. When I was younger, I prioritized friends and family events as the center pieces of my days, like the framed photographs that line my bookshelves today. Everything else was an embellishment floating around those glistening focal points. Over time, each passing milestone has led to more items piling upon the surface:

work notes and business magazines, for example. There's no longer room for air in between the necessary elements of my life—the kind of space needed for beauty to shine through in the light. This imbalance is an unsustainable equation. Cherishing the people in my life and my beloved teacup chihuahua, Coco, goes without saying. Keeping track of myself in the midst of the chaos is another matter.

I think *a lot* about how to use my unclaimed time for maximum impact. I'm, probably much like you, here to make use of my unique gifts. Through my own attempts to achieve big things, I feel I'm able to show potential of what other people are capable of. But this truth competes with a constant melody of unkind voices in my mind that cry:

> *You're not so special.*
> *What makes you think you can make a difference?*
> *This is a waste of your time, your energy.*
> *Just stop before you embarrass yourself.*

Whether soft or booming, these are the phrases I dance around in order to succeed. If you struggle like me, then giving in to internal negativity makes us hostages to our own imaginations. With the worst possible scenarios all playing out at once, we can get pulled into unending vortexes that contort our minds, building walls that block our potential, preventing us from cultivating the splendor we're here to share.

My truest obligation is to take every possible chance to make a splash. Or at least try. My purpose is resisting the downward pull and feed the fire in my unusual soul. Part of that is pursuing curiosity, even if it feels like a waste of my precious time. Each day should be about making room for beauty to shine through. This life is my only moment. I came to do a job, to do positive things. And I won't give in to the mindset of 'If Only.'

If only I had the right credentials.
If only I knew the right people.
If only I didn't have to worry about money.
... Then I would be able to live out my destiny.

'If Only' creates a disposition of defeat. In this space, I'm bent in a hunched-down posture as the world's restrictions press upon me, that is when I can best see the truth: I am the one who can solve the problems that I see.

There's nothing left to do, just get up each time I'm down. Again and again, get on, move—and don't waste life worrying about a pretty landing.

*He who is not courageous enough to take
risks will accomplish nothing in life.*

—MUHAMMAD ALI

FLY

2018 was the year of staking a claim on my life. Bold notions and a surge of fearlessness led me to leave a job that had in many ways defined me. Right away, I found myself diving head-first into a bid for public office. It was the thrill of a lifetime. A campaign set in the dead of winter. Four months of fighting through the slush and the snow—frozen lips while knocking on doors, connecting with people I never knew were my neighbors, and speaking to groups about my ideas for inclusion and equality. I broke free from the stale office air and was able to effectively address problems in my community by using my skills and experience with government programs. It was a new chapter, and I was just excited to be at the party.

This campaign was my big debut to the general public, as well as to the political establishment. I met so many people. I connected with community members who understood my passion for service and unique knowledge of the important issues facing our community. What I enjoyed most was hearing the concerns of voters. We found common elements in our lives and discussed ways to find real solutions to big problems. I had the opportunity to see such enthusiasm for the campaign reflected back on their faces, and that was everything.

The beauty of running for office for the first time is what I would call 'losing your security blanket.' Your deadline is Election Day, and every moment until then matters. There's no time for hesitation or uncertainty. You have to clarify your point of view to voters. It's early mornings and late nights. Every day is a new battle, a new challenge to connect your message to every possible voter. If you're shy, running for office is the ultimate boot camp experience. Any person who you think may be able to vote in your election must be approached with confidence. Then you tell them your name, background, vision for the community, and why you're the best person to deliver for them. For me, this process was transformative. I understood my strengths but had always felt like saying them out loud would be too *braggy*. Just like you, my unique skill set is doing no one any good if I keep it to myself.

On Election Day, the voters chose a different candidate. I thought I was better prepared for any outcome. I knew there was a strong possibility the day would not go my way. But when you put all of yourself into something, it's hard to accept defeat. The minute the votes were counted, I got an overwhelming headache. The piercing sensation through my right eye socket and into my brain was like nothing I'd ever felt before. I could have powered my hometown with the amount of energy I put into that campaign. It was over and I was exhausted.

After a good night of sleep, the headache was gone. I woke up feeling raw, but also grateful for all I'd experienced throughout those four months. Upon reflection, even coming up short on Election Day brought new meaning. I'd never been able to connect with more people and share so much of myself. At the end of it all, I felt brave. You don't learn what you're made of from a life full of daisies and victories. Grit promotes growth.

Running for public office is the best thing that I've ever done. Someone once said that the hardest things are the most essential. As each day ends, it's important for me to know that I've done everything I can to make my contribution. Life is about taking care of each other. A lot of the time, that means building great things together. This takes action, and action requires courage. For me, the question has always been whether I would jump in to make the mark I was destined for or allow others' assumptions to shut me out. Many times, I have chosen the latter.

The perceptions that others impose on us threaten our connection to our own truth. For me, it's being told that I'm "confined" to a wheelchair, disabled and suffering, always expected to be pleasant yet passive. I'm a person with many gifts and talents. It's up to me to navigate my personal obstacles, to be visible and at the table for governmental decision-making processes that affect people like me—people who struggle to be seen because they are consumed with surviving. Much of the time, that means jumping through hoops to maintain the social service programs they depend on. My voice, my observations, and my convictions are the best tools I could ask for.

The window to live out the highest expression of ourselves is closing with each passing day. When you're really living, you can feel it in your stomach—it's a mix of excitement, anxiety, and fear. You get it when you throw yourself into something that you know is right without being assured what the outcome will be. Nothing the world has to say can stop you. There is a sense that today is full of endless possibilities, and we don't know that tomorrow will bring such guaranteed satisfaction.

It's a rush and it's just like flying.

ACKNOWLEDGMENTS

———

This book started out as a straightforward idea to publish some old blog posts I had written, but eventually, evolved into something completely different. The writing process itself has been an exercise in self-exploration and discipline, and I'm so grateful for the opportunity to finally share this material with the world.

A big thanks to Hamar for the perfect design for the book cover. Also, thank you so much to Connie Ward for contributing her amazing talent for the author photo.

Regarding what you find beneath the cover ... Everything I wrote started with reflection. I have had a lot of time to think about the messages I receive from the world around me and how they may impact the vision I have for myself or my potential for future achievement. Putting these thoughts down for the first time also helped clarify some of the individuals who have positively impacted me in a big way, which is how the essays for Ed Roberts and Annie Hopkins came about. It was extremely nerve-racking for me to let anyone read the first draft, and ultimately, this book would have never happened if it wasn't for the generosity of Kelsey Paisley-Lasso. She offered her time and intellect to get me from a very rough draft to a more cohesive collection of essays, and the encouragement to keep going. I will be forever grateful.

Additionally, thank you so much to my editor, Holly Marley-Henschen. She was a rock star at helping me bring the material together and communicate my message more effectively.

There are many references to my team of caregivers in the book. It would be impossible to name all of the individuals who have made a deep impression on me. To those who have cared for me, supported me, and made my life possible – past and present – I can't thank you enough.

I am extremely fortunate to have good friendships in my life as well. Rachel Hermes, thank you for being equal parts analytical and inspirational. Your belief in me and my ideas helps me tremendously. Thank you to Callie Schoate for bringing the steady dose of optimism I always need in my life. Thanks to Liz Armstrong for showing me all the grand possibilities this world has to offer, and to Dale Hopkins for consistently sharing his wisdom and a kind word with me.

My brother, Joel Gouker, who always thinks outside the box and shows me a new perspective I had never considered before. Thank you for expanding my mind every day.

But, most of all, thank you to Elaine Arand, my mother. I have learned more lessons from her than I can count. Through her influence, I know how to be the calm presence in a storm, and that any goal is attainable one step at a time. Many experiences and opportunities have been within my grasp because of her. Thank you, Mom, a million times over.

"... This is the lesson: Never give in. Never give in. Never, never, never, never - in nothing, great or small, large or petty never give in, except to convictions of honour and good sense. Never yield to force. Never yield to the apparently overwhelming might of the enemy."

—Sir Winston Churchill

AUTHOR'S NOTE

―――――

In case you haven't gathered by now, I'm a pretty intense person. My first memory was a time just after my family and I had returned home from visiting my father's 90-year-old grandmother. Before leaving we'd always say something like, "Goodbye, see you soon!" and she'd respond with "I hope not!"—a statement she pulled off as simultaneously grim and spunky. Soon after we got home, I was curled up on my mom's lap. Then it suddenly hit me like a freight train—how fleeting everything is. Old age isn't just something that happened to old people, but aging would be a part of my life and the lives of the rest of my family. Eventually our time on this Earth together would come to an end. My sobs forced out the words, "And I'm already four!"

The truth of mortality struck me again at 33 when I learned that my father had suddenly and unexpectedly passed away. Loss of a parental figure is news that literally everyone will confront at one time or another. Yet, when it's your parent, it feels like the most unnatural concept. It's impossible for me to explain the unique character that was my dad, but here's what I can tell you ...

The night before his high school friends were leaving for college, my father famously decided that perhaps he too wanted to go. He packed some things and drove two hours south to Illinois State University. He crashed on the floor at a high school friend's place for the two weeks it took the university to process his transcript and find him a dorm room. He earned a bachelor's degree in economics and math, then returned to his beloved hometown and never looked back.

A true jack-of-all-trades, he owned a business that had a fluctuating number of specialties but financial planning, tax preparation, and buying and selling stocks were constant in the array of services he provided. After I graduated college, I asked, "What do I tell people when they ask me what you do, Dad?" He didn't have an answer. He wore so many hats. In his spare time, he was a devoted public servant. He was elected to the local school board before serving on the county board of directors, proudly holding the chairman position for a decade. My dad cared about and believed in his community, and he would show up for his friends and neighbors in any way possible.

Growing up with a father who had sizable responsibilities and many commitments, I didn't know where or how I fit into the picture. In my early teens, I accepted the idea that he would forever be an ominous figure sitting at the edges of my story.

But, as the beating pulse of teenage angst died down, I got to know myself better as an adult. It became undeniable that, in many ways, my dad and I were exactly the same. Both of my parents raised me to find ways to be of service to others, to do whatever I could to share my God-given talents with my community and those closest to me. It was the intensity with which my dad approached everything that I began to recognize as an intrinsic part of me. His passion for politics was contagious. Every election I can remember was, for him, a question between an America meeting its glorious promise of democracy or the absolute end of America's greatness. Over time, our perspectives differed regarding what constituted a political victory. But we always talked politics. I so loved to get his take on the issues that were in the national spotlight.

One of the things I respected most about my dad was his clearly defined beliefs. He always knew exactly where he stood on any topic, even when everyone else in the room disagreed with his perspective. For instance, he hated public libraries. I love them. It was fascinating for me to watch as he would work himself into such a frenzy talking about libraries as a misuse of public funds, "because there was already an abundance of free information on the internet." When I was in my early 20s, the library board in my hometown started planning to build a bigger and better library. My dad was outraged. He supported the pursuit of knowledge for all people, but he felt strongly that the board wasn't going through the appropriate process of public consideration and open meetings before moving ahead with their plans. So, he led the charge for the resistance. He wrote one letter to the editor after another, explaining his point of view, why following a process before using public funds is so important for any civil society. "It's about respect," he said.

They ended up building the library—right in front of his house.

My dad was a very private person, a bit mysterious in many ways. But he was a man of great principle and that was clear for all to see. He purposely arranged his work meetings so that he could drive his lifelong friend to her cancer treatments. He never missed an opportunity to honor a fallen service member from our community. He stood for fairness in his work as a public servant. He saw every situation in a historical context—he wrote countless "This Day in History" posts on Facebook. He modeled the importance of critical thinking and showed me that developing one's personal belief system is a sacred part of life. He felt it was his duty to share his point of view—especially when everyone else saw things differently—and he instilled that same instinct in me.

If it wasn't for Kim Patrick Gouker, I wouldn't have run for public office. It was he who motivated me to do it in the first place. Sitting on my living room couch, he explained that my unique perspective needed to be part of the conversation to better my community. I hadn't considered it before our conversation, but I knew he was right. He was behind the scenes, supporting me and cheering me on every step of the way. I will forever cherish that chapter of my life, for what I discovered about myself, as well as the closeness I felt with my dad. There's no myth surrounding his memory, but to me, he will always be a legend.

In my quiet moments, when I am wondering if he's hovering around me like a friendly Casper the Ghost-like creature, I focus on the lessons I learned from him. My father helped light the fire that burns inside me today. There's so much work left to do. Still ringing in my ears is the way my dad would close each conversation we had during my political campaign:

"Anner, we're doing this!"